THE
AUTO ACCIDENT
PLAYBOOK

THE GUIDE THE INSURANCE COMPANIES DON'T WANT YOU TO HAVE

ATTORNEY ROBERT SEARS & DR. WENDY SCHAUER

COPYRIGHT 2025

All Rights Reserved

Paperback ISBN: 979-8-9889786-5-7
Ebook ISBN: 979-8-9889786-6-4

DISCLAIMER

ENDORSEMENTS

"The Sears Law Firm exceeded my expectations. From day one, they made a traumatic experience easier to navigate. I knew going up against a big insurance company would feel like David vs. Goliath—but with Sears on my side, I didn't feel alone. Even though the other driver was at fault, the insurance company only offered $50,000. Thanks to the hard work and dedication of the team at Sears, they secured a $200,000 settlement for my injuries. I'm a proud and grateful client, and I know they'll fight just as hard for you."

— Jamie Herrick

"Sears Injury Law represented me after my March 2024 car accident, and I couldn't be more impressed. Their Puyallup team went above and beyond to keep me informed, supported, and confident every step of the way. They were professional, compassionate, and highly skilled—and thanks to their dedication, I secured a result that exceeded my expectations. I'm truly grateful for everything they did. If you need a personal injury attorney who delivers, I highly recommend Sears Injury Law."

— Brenda Riley

"Rob Sears and his incredible team have become my team. From being rear-ended on I-5 to holding a school district accountable, they consistently put our best interests first. At every step, Sears Injury Law prioritized my well-being, recovery, and livelihood. They made sure the responsible parties were held fully accountable for the impact on my life. The compassion, respect, and personal attention I received were truly unmatched. I was always kept informed and treated like family, not just another case. That experience is why I've returned for representation and confidently referred friends and family, knowing they would receive the same exceptional care and commitment to justice. We are deeply grateful for everything Sears Injury Law has done for us and those we love."

— Jason Gilbertson

"I've had the pleasure of knowing Dr. Wendy Schauer, D.C., for nearly 30 years, and she is truly a cornerstone of the chiropractic community. As the former President of the South Sound Chiropractic Association, Dr. Schauer has led with integrity, wisdom, and an unwavering commitment to patient care. She consistently goes above and beyond - advocating for her patients, guiding them through complex systems, and delivering compassionate, results-driven care. She's the kind of doctor who makes you proud to be part of this profession."

— Dr. Mitchell Derrick, B.A., D.C.

"After my motorcycle accident, I was completely lost. Then I found Dr. Wendy Schauer, D.C. She didn't just treat my injuries - she guided me through every step, from recovery to legal help. For two years, she made sure I had the right care, the right team, and the right outcome. My body healed, my case was resolved, and I never had to face it alone. Dr. Schauer is the reason I got my life back."

— Eric W., Motorcycle Collision Survivor

"Dr. Wendy Schauer, D.C., is truly one of the greats. As a Chiropractic Physician, she provides exceptional care, and I regularly refer my patients to her. What truly sets her apart is who she is beyond the clinic. She is genuine, enthusiastic, and a consistent example to those around her. Her dedication to her patients and our healthcare community is unmatched. I am proud to work alongside her and grateful to have her as a trusted colleague."

— Dr. Aaron Utterback, D.P.M.

CONTENTS

FOREWORD

By Kevin Hogan, Psy.D.

When life goes sideways, really sideways, you quickly realize that fixing it is rarely simple. Customer service has turned into customer resistance. It's hard enough to find someone who says they're on your side—even harder to find someone who actually is.

I was chatting with Dr. Wendy Schauer not long ago, and the subject turned to her co-author. "Why this project with Rob Sears?" I asked.

She didn't miss a beat: "Because Rob doesn't just fight for his clients. He goes to war for them. He's tired of seeing good people get taken advantage of after a car crash."

As we talked, I learned more about Rob—his integrity, his charitable work, the depth of his commitment. I walked away not just impressed, but genuinely relieved that she found the perfect partner to create something like this.

Then I read the book.

And let me tell you something: this isn't just a book. It's a blueprint. A roadmap for one of life's worst-case scenarios. A practical guide for when the unthinkable happens—a motor vehicle collision, and someone you love is hurt.

Most people think they know what to do: exchange insurance, don't admit fault. That's about it, right? Wrong. You have *no idea* what you don't know until you're in the middle of it.

Flip to any page in this book. You'll learn things that seem counterintuitive - like calling the fire department instead of just an ambulance. You'll be guided through building a small but mighty recovery team, starting with a skilled attorney and a practitioner who truly understands how the body heals.

This book doesn't belong on your bookshelf. It belongs in your glove box. And maybe a second copy on your coffee table, so your friends and family can read it *before* they need it.

I've known Dr. Schauer for 15 years. As someone who's been skeptical of chiropractors, let me say this: Wendy is the real deal. When I had a fall in Las Vegas, she showed up with her husband, taped me up like a scientist in action, and got me through it. Since then, I've heard story after story of her going the extra mile for her patients.

And now, with this book? She and Rob are going the extra mile for *you*. Read it. Mark it up. Share it.

Because when life hits you hard, you want people in your corner who know exactly what to do.

You just found them.

DEDICATION

To those whose lives have been turned upside down by a car crash, and who are doing their best to pick up the pieces. This is for you.

From Rob

To every client who's trusted me to stand by them in their darkest hour—thank you. You've taught me more about courage than I could ever teach in return.

From Wendy

To my patients, who let me walk beside them as they heal. You remind me daily that recovery is both a science and an art. Thank you for trusting me.

PREFACE

Life has a way of knocking the wind out of us. One minute you're driving to work or picking up groceries, and the next – CRASH! It feels like everything shatters: your plans, your sense of control, maybe even your body.

We wrote this book for that moment. For *you*. Whether you've just been in a motor vehicle collision or you're reading this because you want to be prepared, know this: you're not alone.

We're Rob and Wendy. One of us is a personal injury attorney who's spent years helping people stand up to insurance companies and legal red tape. The other is a chiropractor who has spent decades helping people literally get back on their feet.

We teamed up for one reason: to help people get through one of the most difficult experiences of their lives—physically, emotionally, legally, and financially.

This book is more than a how-to. It's a guide to making smart decisions when it feels like the ground is shifting under your feet. We'll walk you through the essential steps you need to take, from the first moments after a crash to your long-term healing and recovery.

You'll learn what to do, what *not* to do, and who to call. You'll get honest advice, real stories, and tools that can make all the difference.

And maybe most importantly, you'll be reminded that you have more strength than you think. Let us show you the way.

With care,

Attorney Robert Sears & Dr. Wendy Schauer

CHAPTER 1

BEFORE IT HAPPENS - WHY YOUR INSURANCE COVERAGE MATTERS MORE THAN YOU THINK

Let's Talk About the Boring Stuff—Before It Becomes the Big Stuff

Auto insurance. Just the phrase probably makes your eyes glaze over. Most of us think of it as a necessary evil—something we pay for, hope we never use, and kind of ignore until something goes wrong.

But here's the hard truth: when a motor vehicle collision happens, your insurance coverage isn't just a piece of paper. It's the difference between recovery and ruin.

You might be thinking, *I'm a safe driver, I've never had a crash, I don't need all that extra stuff.* But insurance isn't for when everything goes right. It's for when someone else runs a red light. It's for when life sideswipes you—literally.

In this chapter, we're going to walk you through why having the *right* coverage *before* a collision is one of the smartest, most protective moves you can make. We're not trying to scare you. We're trying to *prepare* you.

STEP 1: Research the Right Insurance Company

All insurance is not created equal. You want a company that will actually show up when it counts. Not one that ghosts you when the bill comes due.

Here's what to look for:

- ▸ **Coverage Options That Actually Cover You**: Make sure your policy includes liability, collision, comprehensive, and uninsured/underinsured motorist coverage. Ask questions. Know what each line on that policy actually means.

- ▸ **Financial Strength**: Look up their rating on sites like A.M. Best. A strong rating means they're financially stable and more likely to pay out fairly.

- ▸ **Claims Reputation**: Read reviews. Check J.D. Power rankings. Ask people you trust. You want a company that pays *quickly* and *fairly*, not one known for dragging its feet.

Real Talk Example: Imagine you're in a wreck. You're hurt, your car is totaled, and your medical bills are climbing. The last thing you want is to be stuck in a battle with your insurer. Choose one now who fights *for* you, not against you.

STEP 2: Build a Relationship With a Local Agent

Online-only companies might be cheap, but they won't sit across from you at a coffee shop and explain what "UM/UIM" means. A good local agent can be your advocate before, during, and after an accident.

Why it matters:

▶ They get to know *you* and your real-life situation.

▶ They can help tailor your policy to your actual needs.

▶ If something goes wrong, you know who to call—and they know you.

Example: Say you upgrade your car to one with fancy tech and safety features. A good agent might suggest adding gap insurance so you're not stuck owing thousands if it's totaled. That kind of foresight can save you big.

STEP 3: Don't Shop Only on Price

It's tempting, especially with all the ads, to just pick the cheapest premium. But cheap can be very, *very* expensive later.

When comparing policies, look at:

▶ Claims handling speed

▶ 24/7 support availability

▶ Online tools and apps (like for roadside assistance)

▶ Bundle discounts (home + auto, etc.)

▶ Coverage limits (higher is better!)

Remember: insurance is about *protection*, not price tags.

STEP 4: Know the Consequences of Being Underinsured

Let's say you carry the bare minimum required by law. It might seem fine—until you get in a serious crash.

If your coverage is too low:

▶ You could be personally responsible for tens (or hundreds) of thousands of dollars.

▶ Your wages could be garnished.

▶ You might have to sell assets.

Example: Someone with state-minimum $25k liability limits crashes into another car. That car has two passengers with $80,000 in combined medical bills. Guess who's on the hook for the other $55,000? You.

STEP 5: Protect Your Future Self

Insurance is one of those things that doesn't seem important—until it's the *only* thing that matters. By doing your homework, getting proper coverage, and connecting with someone you trust, you're giving your future self a lifeline.

You might never need it. We sincerely hope you don't. But if you do? You'll be so glad you didn't cut corners.

Peace of mind doesn't come from luck. It comes from preparation.

Next up: what to do in the *minutes* after a collision. Because once it happens, everything moves fast. And the first steps matter more than most people realize.

Let's make sure you're ready.

CHAPTER 2

MOMENTS AFTER IMPACT - WHAT TO DO RIGHT AFTER THE COLLISION

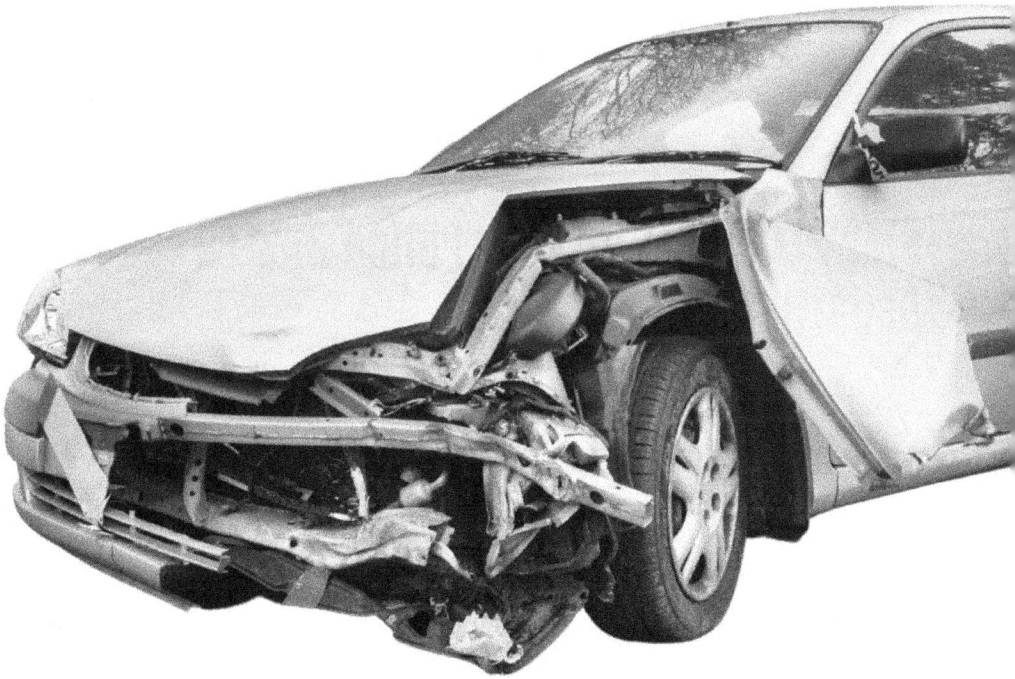

The First Ten Minutes Matter

It happens fast. A slam. A jolt. Tires screech. Then silence. You're shaken, maybe confused, maybe hurt. But what you do in the next few minutes could have a lasting impact on your health, your finances, and even your legal case.

Let's slow it down.

You don't need to panic. You need a plan. This chapter is your plan.

STEP 1: Check Yourself and Your Passengers

Take a deep breath. Your heart might be racing. Do a quick self-scan: Can you move? Are you bleeding? Is anyone in your car unconscious or clearly injured?

Even if you feel "fine," remember: shock masks pain. Injuries like whiplash or concussions might not show up until hours or days later.

Stay calm. Stay present. Help others if you can, but don't put yourself in further danger.

STEP 2: Call 911–Ask for Police *and* Fire Department

This is where most people get it wrong. They call for an ambulance if someone's hurt, or just the police for a report. But here's the trick:

Always ask for the fire department too.

Why? Firefighters often arrive faster. They're trained in trauma and emergency care. And their documentation can become a powerful part of your case if things get complicated later.

Say it clearly: *"We've been in a car crash. We need police, fire, and medical if available."*

STEP 3: Stay in Your Vehicle Unless It's Unsafe

Unless you smell gas, see fire, or your car is in a dangerous spot (like the middle of an intersection), don't rush out.

You could have spinal injuries. Getting out and walking around may worsen the damage—and it might even hurt your legal case if you appear "fine" to witnesses or cameras.

Stay put. Turn on your hazard lights. Take slow, deep breaths.

STEP 4: Document Everything—But Don't Say Too Much

When it's safe, start gathering evidence. Here's your checklist:

- ▷ Take photos of all vehicles, damage, license plates, and the surrounding scene
- ▷ Get names and contact info of witnesses
- ▷ Record names and badge numbers of responding officers
- ▷ Screenshot traffic, weather, and nearby businesses with cameras

But be careful what you say. Don't admit fault. Don't say, *"I'm okay."* Just stick to facts. Anything you say can be used against you.

STEP 5: Go to the Hospital or See a Chiropractor Immediately

Even if you think you're okay, get checked out. Emergency rooms rule out serious injuries. Chiropractors specialize in the soft-tissue damage that ERs often overlook.

Insurance companies look at how fast you sought treatment. Waiting even a few days gives them ammo to say you weren't really hurt.

Your body comes first. Always.

STEP 6: Call an Attorney Before You Call Your Insurance

This surprises people, but it's crucial: speak to an experienced personal injury attorney *before* you call your insurance company.

Why? Because insurance adjusters work for the company—not for you. Their job is to settle fast and cheap.

An attorney protects your rights from the start. Many offer free consultations. It costs you nothing to have someone in your corner from Day One.

What NOT to Do:

- ▶▶ Don't apologize, even politely.
- ▶▶ Don't tell anyone you feel fine.
- ▶▶ Don't post about the crash on social media.
- ▶▶ Don't delay medical care.
- ▶▶ Don't give a recorded statement without legal advice.

The Aftershock Will Come—But You'll Be Ready

You'll feel overwhelmed. That's normal. But now you've got a plan.

This is where your recovery begins—with the choices you make *right now*.

Next chapter? We'll guide you through the next 24 to 48 hours. Because healing and justice both start with smart steps.

We've got you.

CHAPTER 3

AFTER THE DUST SETTLES - THE NEXT 48 HOURS

You Survived the Crash. Now What?

The adrenaline fades. The pain starts to creep in. Maybe you're sore, stiff, or just shaken. The next day or two are critical—not just for your health, but for setting the stage for the rest of your recovery.

This is when you're most vulnerable. It's easy to think, *I'll wait and see if it gets better.* But waiting is what insurance companies are counting on.

Here's what you need to know and do in the first 48 hours.

STEP 1: Get Thorough Medical Attention (Again)

If you didn't go to the hospital right after the crash, now is the time. If you did, but you're feeling worse—or even if you're feeling "okay"—book a follow-up.

Don't ignore new symptoms like:

- ▶▶ Headaches
- ▶▶ Dizziness
- ▶▶ Neck or back pain
- ▶▶ Numbness or tingling
- ▶▶ Trouble concentrating

These could be signs of concussions, soft tissue injuries, or even internal damage. Better to catch it now.

STEP 2: Start a Healing Log

Buy a notebook or open a notes app. Every day, jot down:

- ▶▶ Your pain level (1–10)
- ▶▶ What hurts
- ▶▶ What you're unable to do

- ▶ Medications you took
- ▶ Appointments attended

Why? Because weeks from now, you may forget how bad it was at the beginning. A written log gives your attorney proof and your providers context.

STEP 3: Follow All Medical Advice

If a doctor tells you to rest, rest. If they refer you to a chiropractor, go. If they suggest imaging, get it done.

Insurance adjusters *love* to see gaps in care. They'll argue, "If you didn't follow up, you must not be that hurt."

Show up. Stick with it. Your consistency proves the pain is real.

STEP 4: Tell Your Employer - Briefly and Professionally

Even if you plan to power through work, it's smart to notify your employer that you were in a crash. This creates a paper trail in case you need time off later.

Keep it short: *"I wanted to inform you that I was involved in a motor vehicle collision and will be receiving follow-up care. I will keep you updated if anything affects my work schedule."*

STEP 5: Track All Expenses

Create a folder—digital or physical. Save every receipt, bill, and statement related to:

- ▶ Medical visits
- ▶ Prescriptions

- ▶ Transportation or towing
- ▶ Car rental or repairs
- ▶ Missed workdays

These add up. Every dollar matters in a personal injury case.

STEP 6: Protect Your Peace

You're likely feeling overwhelmed, emotional, and unsure. That's normal. Here's what helps:

- ▶ Ask a friend or partner to help with paperwork or errands
- ▶ Get extra rest - your body is healing
- ▶ Limit screen time and doom-scrolling
- ▶ Avoid speaking with the other driver's insurance

Most importantly, remember: you're not crazy. Collisions are traumatic. The emotional impact is just as real as the physical one.

The Next Chapter Is About Rebuilding

The first 48 hours are about stabilizing and documenting. What comes next? Building your recovery team—and making sure the people around you are truly on *your* side.

We'll walk you through how to find a chiropractor who works with your attorney, and how both can become your most powerful allies.

You've made it through the hardest part. Now let's rebuild…together.

CHAPTER 4

BUILDING YOUR RECOVERY TEAM - FINDING THE RIGHT CHIROPRACTOR AND ATTORNEY

You Don't Have to Heal Alone

The crash is behind you, but the journey to healing has just begun. And let's be honest—it can be a lonely road. Pain, paperwork, confusion about who to trust… it all piles up fast.

That's why your next step is building a *team*—not just any team, but one that's laser-focused on helping you recover, inside and out. The two most important people on that team?

Your chiropractor. And your attorney.

This chapter is your guide to finding the right ones.

STEP 1: Why a Chiropractor Can Be a Lifeline

Most people think chiropractors only help with back pain. But after a motor vehicle collision, a good chiropractor can help your body heal at the root level, especially when it comes to soft- tissue injuries, whiplash, joint misalignment, and nerve irritation.

Chiropractic care isn't just about pain relief. It's about:

- ▶ Restoring function
- ▶ Reducing inflammation
- ▶ Preventing long-term damage
- ▶ Helping you return to work and daily life

Think of it like this: after a crash, your spine and muscles are like a house that's been shaken by an earthquake. A chiropractor helps to realign the foundation before cracks get worse.

STEP 2: What to Look for in a Chiropractor

Not all chiropractors are created equal. Here's what to look for:

▶ **Experience with Personal Injury Cases**: Ask if they've treated motor vehicle collision patients before. They should understand how to document your injuries in a way that supports your case.

▶ **Willingness to Refer Out**: A great chiropractor isn't afraid to say, "You need a neurologist, massage therapist, or acupuncturist too." That's a good sign they're thinking about *your* health, not just their calendar.

▶ **Open Communication**: You want someone who explains your diagnosis and treatment plan clearly. No guessing, no jargon.

Bonus: If your chiropractor and attorney know each other—or at least communicate—that's a huge win. It means they can coordinate care and paperwork to support your case.

STEP 3: The Attorney Who Actually Fights for You

There's a huge difference between a personal injury attorney who just files paperwork—and one who *fights*. You want the fighter.

The right attorney will:

▶ Protect you from predatory insurance companies

▶ Help you get compensated fairly for pain, suffering, lost wages, and more

▶ Guide you through every legal step so you can focus on healing

And no, you don't need to pay upfront. Most personal injury attorneys work on a contingency fee - meaning they only get paid if you win.

STEP 4: How to Find the Right Attorney

Here are the green flags to look for:

- **Specializes in Personal Injury**: Not all lawyers do. Ask how many car crash cases they've handled *this year*.
- **Available and Responsive**: If you're always getting voicemail or feel rushed, keep looking.
- **Clear and Honest**: A good attorney tells you the truth, even if it's not what you want to hear. They won't overpromise.
- **Team-Oriented**: Ask if they've worked with chiropractors before. If they have a network of trusted providers, that's a major plus.

Pro tip: Ask your chiropractor who they recommend. They often know which attorneys are truly patient-focused—and which ones to avoid.

STEP 5: Red Flags to Avoid in Both

Here's what to steer clear of:

- Anyone who guarantees a huge settlement (no one can)
- Providers who treat every patient the same, without a tailored plan
- Offices that feel like mills—churning patients in and out, fast
- Lawyers who push you to settle quickly or avoid medical care You deserve more than a "quick fix." You deserve a real recovery.

STEP 6: Trust Your Gut

You're the one living in your body. You're the one walking through the aftermath of this crash. So, if a provider makes you feel rushed, dismissed, or uneasy? Move on.

Your body and your future are too important.

Find the chiropractor who sees you as a whole person, not just a spine. Find the attorney who answers your questions and makes you feel protected.

They're out there. And when you find them, healing gets a whole lot easier.

Up Next: Understanding the Types of Coverage That Can Actually Protect You

Let's talk about the acronyms that matter most—PIP, UM, UIM—and how they could be the difference between bouncing back or going broke.

Ready? Let's go protect your future.

CHAPTER 5

THE HIDDEN LIFELINES – WHAT PIP, UM, AND UIM COVERAGE REALLY MEAN FOR YOU

Acronyms That Can Save You Thousands

We get it. Insurance terms like PIP, UM, and UIM sound like alphabet soup. But here's the deal: these three coverages could be the difference between you making a full recovery or drowning in debt.

They're called "add-ons," but don't be fooled, they're essentials. In this chapter, we'll break down what these coverages mean, why they matter more than most people realize, and how to make sure you're fully protected.

Let's decode the fine print.

STEP 1: What Is PIP and Why You Absolutely Need It

PIP stands for *Personal Injury Protection*. Think of it as your go-to coverage when the chaos hits. It kicks in *immediately* after a collision, no matter who was at fault.

Here's what PIP typically covers:

▶ Medical bills (chiropractic care, ER visits, imaging, prescriptions)

▶ Lost wages

▶ Transportation to and from medical appointments

▶ Help with housework or childcare if you're too injured to do them

The best part? You don't have to wait for the insurance companies to figure out fault. PIP gets you help *now*.

Most states require only the bare minimum - often just a few thousand dollars. But you can usually purchase up to $35,000 or more. That extra cushion can mean fewer bills and more peace of mind.

STEP 2: UM and UIM Coverage - The Unsung Heroes

Let's say the driver who hit you doesn't have insurance. Or they have the state minimum—just enough to legally drive, but nowhere near enough to cover your injuries.

That's where UM and UIM come in:

- ▶▶ **UM (Uninsured Motorist)**: Covers *you* if the other driver has *no* insurance.
- ▶▶ **UIM (Underinsured Motorist)**: Covers the gap when the other driver's insurance doesn't cover all your damages.

These coverages protect *you*. And yet, they're often left off to save a few bucks a month. Truth bomb? Skipping UM/UIM is like skydiving without a backup parachute.

STEP 3: The Real-Life Difference These Make

Here's a true story (names changed):

Sarah was rear-ended by a distracted driver. Her medical bills hit $42,000. The at-fault driver had the state minimum—just $25,000 in liability coverage. Without UIM, Sarah would've been stuck paying the $17,000 difference out of pocket.

But Sarah had UIM.

Her policy kicked in and covered the gap. She didn't go into debt. She kept her house. She kept her peace.

That's the power of being prepared.

STEP 4: How Much Coverage Should You Have?

We recommend this baseline:

- ▶ **PIP**: $25,000 minimum (more if you can)
- ▶ **UM/UIM**: Match your liability limits. If you have $100k in liability coverage, get $100k in UM/UIM too.

Why? Because you can't control other people's decisions. But you can absolutely protect yourself.

The good news? Adding this coverage is usually surprisingly affordable.

STEP 5: Call Your Insurance Agent Today

This isn't one of those "I'll get around to it next week" things. Call your agent and ask:

- ▶ Do I have PIP? How much?
- ▶ Do I have UM and UIM? What are the limits?
- ▶ How much would it cost to increase them?

You might be shocked how little extra protection costs.

STEP 6: Why This Matters Now More Than Ever

Medical costs are rising. More drivers are uninsured. Crashes are happening every day. And when it happens to *you*, it won't matter what your premium used to be. It will only matter what you *actually have*.

Let this be your safety net. Your backup plan. Your armor.

Protect your body. Protect your finances. Protect your peace of mind.

Coming Up: Who Pays What and When - How Coverage Actually Works After a Crash

Now that you understand the types of coverage, let's walk through what happens when the bills start rolling in. Who pays first? What does your insurance cover? What if it isn't enough?

Let's take the confusion out of claims, step by step.

CHAPTER 6

WHO PAYS WHAT AND WHEN - DEMYSTIFYING THE CLAIMS PROCESS

The Bill Comes Due—Now What?

You've been through the crash, you've gotten care, you've notified the right people. But now the bills are arriving, and it can feel like you've been hit all over again—this time by paperwork, phone calls, and dollar signs.

Let's take the mystery and stress out of it. In this chapter, we'll walk you through who pays what, when they pay, and what to do if coverage isn't enough.

STEP 1: Understand the Order of Coverage

Right after a collision, a few insurance coverages may apply at once. Here's the general order:

- ▶▶ PIP (Personal Injury Protection) pays first.
- ▶▶ Health Insurance may kick in after PIP is exhausted.
- ▶▶ UM/UIM Coverage fills in if the at-fault driver's policy isn't enough.
- ▶▶ The At-Fault Driver's Liability Insurance eventually covers your damages (but it can take time).

The key? **PIP is your first line of defense.**

It covers medical expenses, some lost wages, and transportation costs regardless of who caused the crash. Once PIP runs out, your health insurance or other policies may start contributing.

STEP 2: Expect Delays from the At-Fault Driver's Insurance

It may seem obvious that the person who hit you should pay right away. Unfortunately, it doesn't work that fast.

Why? Their insurance company has to:

- ⯮ Investigate the claim
- ⯮ Determine fault
- ⯮ Review medical records
- ⯮ Negotiate

This can take *weeks* or even *months*. That's why your own coverage (like PIP) is so important, it bridges the gap.

STEP 3: Your Attorney Is Your Claims Bodyguard

You should not be navigating this alone. A good personal injury attorney will:

- ⯮ Talk to all the insurance companies for you
- ⯮ Ensure paperwork is submitted on time
- ⯮ Prevent lowball offers or denied claims
- ⯮ Build your case with solid documentation

They know the games insurance adjusters play—and how to counter them. Let them carry that burden while you heal.

STEP 4: Track Every Penny

Keep a folder (or digital file) for:

- ⯮ Medical bills
- ⯮ Mileage and transportation receipts
- ⯮ Missed work documentation
- ⯮ Insurance statements
- ⯮ Notes from appointments

Every expense matters. The more proof you have, the stronger your case for full compensation.

STEP 5: Be Prepared for Subrogation

This part surprises most people. Let's break it down:

If your health insurance pays for treatment, and you later receive a settlement, they may ask to be reimbursed. This is called **subrogation.**

It feels unfair - but it's common. Your attorney will often negotiate this amount down, so you don't lose your entire settlement to paybacks.

STEP 6: What If the Insurance Isn't Enough?

If your medical bills are higher than what the at-fault driver's insurance covers, and you don't have enough UM/UIM coverage, you may be:

- ▶ Responsible for the difference
- ▶ Eligible to file a lawsuit against the at-fault driver (if they have assets)

This is why stacking coverage (PIP + UM/UIM + health insurance) is crucial. Once a collision happens, it's too late to adjust your policy.

You're Not Alone in This

The claims process can be a slow and sometimes frustrating ride. But you're not powerless. With the right team, clear documentation, and strong coverage, you *can* come out the other side whole.

Breathe. Focus on healing. Let the professionals do the rest.

Coming Up: What a Chiropractor Really Does After a Crash

Let's explore what to expect from chiropractic care, what makes a great provider, and how your chiropractor and attorney can work together for your recovery.

You deserve to feel better. Let's get into how that happens.

CHAPTER 7

WHAT A CHIROPRACTOR REALLY DOES AFTER A CRASH - YOUR BODY'S RECOVERY PARTNER

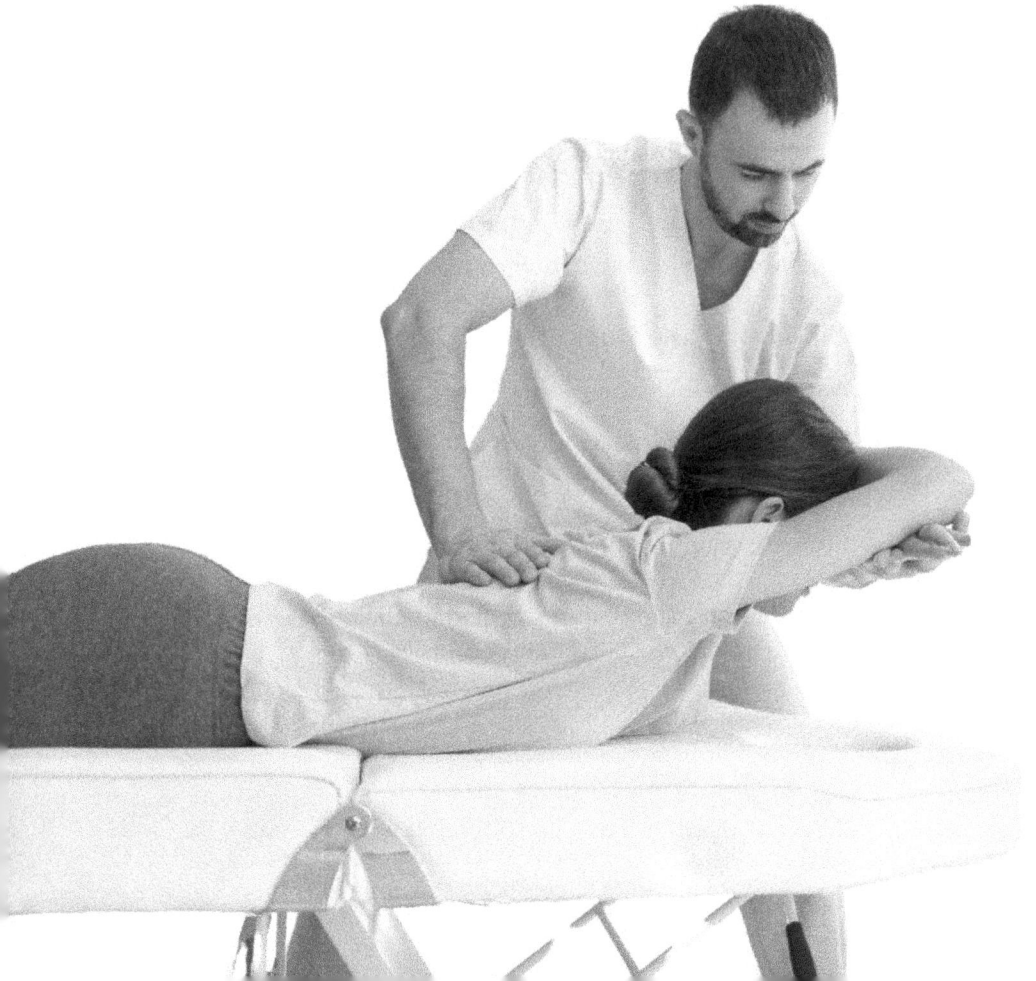

It's Not Just About Your Spine—It's About Your Life

After a collision, most people go straight to the ER. That's a smart first step. But emergency rooms are designed to rule out life-threatening issues—not to help you heal from the pain that lingers for weeks, months, or longer.

That's where chiropractic care comes in.

This chapter is your guide to understanding how a skilled chiropractor becomes one of your most valuable allies after a crash—and what to look out for to make sure you're in the right hands.

STEP 1: Why Chiropractic Care Is Crucial After a Collision

Motor vehicle collisions don't just jolt your car—they jolt your body. Even at low speeds, your musculoskeletal system absorbs an intense amount of force.

The result? Misalignments, muscle spasms, inflammation, pinched nerves, and reduced mobility. Here's what chiropractic care can help with:

- ▶ Whiplash and neck pain
- ▶ Lower back pain
- ▶ Shoulder and joint issues
- ▶ Headaches and migraines
- ▶ Numbness, tingling, or radiating pain

Even if the pain doesn't show up immediately, these issues can snowball into chronic problems if left untreated.

STEP 2: What to Expect From Your First Visits

A good chiropractor will take the time to:

- Review your history and how the crash happened
- Perform a detailed exam
- Possibly refer you out for X-rays or MRIs
- Build a customized treatment plan

You should never feel rushed. Your visits should focus on real healing, not quick fixes. Treatment may include:

- Gentle adjustments
- Soft tissue therapy or muscle work
- Electrical stimulation or ultrasound
- At-home stretches or movement tips

STEP 3: Red Flags to Watch Out For

Unfortunately, not every provider has your best interest in mind. Here are signs that it might be time to switch chiropractors:

- You're given the same treatment every time, with no adjustment to your condition
- You feel pressured to sign a long-term care contract
- They don't communicate with your attorney (or don't know how)
- They refuse to refer you out to specialists even when necessary

Great chiropractors work *with* other providers. They collaborate. They educate. And they respect your right to ask questions.

STEP 4: Your Chiropractor and Attorney Should Be a Team

When your chiropractor and attorney communicate, you win. They can:

- ▶ Coordinate your care timeline with your legal case
- ▶ Ensure that all records, charts, and notes support your claim
- ▶ Avoid treatment gaps that insurers love to point out

Your recovery becomes smoother. Your case becomes stronger.

If your chiropractor has worked with personal injury attorneys before, that's a big plus. Ask them.

STEP 5: You Are an Active Part of Your Recovery

Your chiropractor will guide you—but your participation matters.

What you can do:

- ▶ Show up for all your appointments
- ▶ Follow home-care instructions
- ▶ Track your symptoms in a notebook or app
- ▶ Communicate openly if something isn't working

Healing takes time. It's not always linear. But consistent care adds up—and often makes the difference between a full recovery and lingering pain.

You Deserve a Provider Who Sees You, Hears You, and Helps You Heal

After a crash, you're vulnerable. You need more than pain relief. You need someone who understands the emotional toll, the legal chaos, and the physical discomfort.

That's what a great chiropractor provides: a space to heal, a plan to move forward, and a partner in your recovery.

Coming Up: Bonus Tools to Keep in Your Trunk - How to Prepare for the Unexpected

Let's get practical. What should you have in your car *before* the next crash? We'll walk you through the must-have items that could save you time, stress, and pain later.

CHAPTER 8

BONUS TOOLS TO KEEP IN YOUR TRUNK - HOW TO PREPARE FOR THE UNEXPECTED

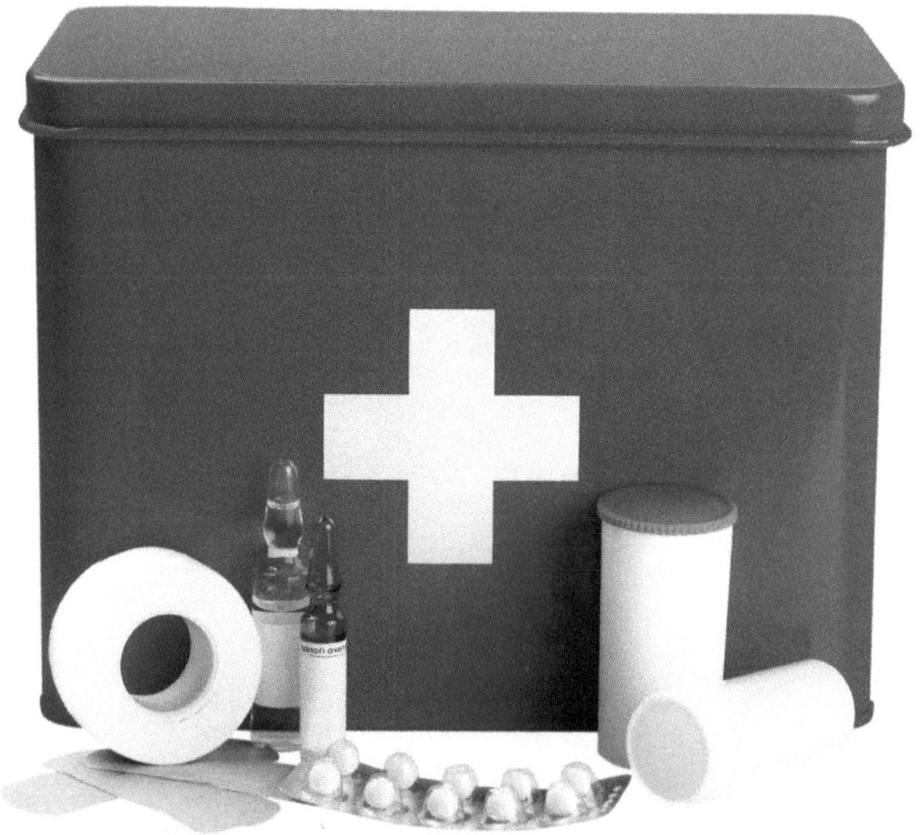

Because Prepared Beats Panicked—Every Time

Nobody expects to get into a crash. But when it happens, those who stay calm and organized tend to come out of it better—physically, emotionally, and financially.

One of the smartest ways to stack the odds in your favor? Keep a well-stocked emergency kit in your trunk.

This isn't about fear. It's about *readiness*.

Let's build your trunk toolkit together.

STEP 1: The Non-Negotiables

These are the items every vehicle should carry:

- ▶ **First Aid Kit** – Bandages, gauze, alcohol wipes, antiseptic, tweezers, gloves, and a CPR mask.
- ▶ **Flashlight with Extra Batteries** – Crashes don't wait for daylight.
- ▶ **Reflective Warning Triangles or Flares** – Keeps you visible if you're stuck on the road.
- ▶ **Blanket or Emergency Foil Blanket** – Especially important during cold weather or shock.
- ▶ **Multi-tool or Swiss Army Knife** – Compact and incredibly useful.
- ▶ **Phone Charger or Battery Pack** – To make calls or take photos after a crash.
- ▶ **Gloves and Poncho** – For bad weather or messy situations.
- ▶ **Pen and Notepad** – To jot down witness info or accident details.
- ▶ **Disposable Camera** – In the event your phone is lost, broken, or dead, a simple disposable camera gives you a reliable backup to document the scene, vehicle damage, road conditions, and even injuries. Physical photos can serve as crucial evidence later, and these cameras are still sold at most drug stores or online.

STEP 2: The Smart Add-Ons

If you've got the space, these extras can be game changers:

- ▶ **Small Fire Extinguisher** – Rated for vehicle use.
- ▶ **Window Breaker and Seatbelt Cutter** – Many combine both in one tool.
- ▶ **Reusable Water Bottle** – Hydration is key after trauma.
- ▶ **Snacks (Non-Perishable)** – Think protein bars or trail mix.
- ▶ **Tire Pressure Gauge and Air Pump** – Especially helpful in remote areas.
- ▶ **Duct Tape** – Trust us, you'll thank yourself later.

STEP 3: Emergency Documents Folder

Keep a waterproof envelope with:

- ▶ Copy of your insurance card
- ▶ Medical contact info and allergies
- ▶ Emergency contact numbers
- ▶ A list of medications you take
- ▶ This book's quick crash checklist (tear-out or printed)

Having this ready saves critical time—and it helps first responders help *you*.

STEP 4: Prepare for Emotional Support Too

Most people focus on physical gear—but emotional grounding tools can be just as important in a high-stress situation.

Why? Because after a crash, your nervous system can go into overdrive. Simple sensory inputs can help calm your brain, regulate your breathing, and bring you back to center. This isn't "woo- woo"—it's backed by neuroscience.

Consider adding:

- A calming essential oil roller (lavender and peppermint have been shown to reduce anxiety and ease tension)
- A stress ball or smooth stone for tactile grounding
- A handwritten note that says: *"You're okay. Breathe. Help is coming."* (This activates the rational part of your brain when emotions are high)

You might be surprised how these simple items can anchor you in the moment and help you take calm, clear action—when it matters most.

STEP 5: Keep It All in a Grab-and-Go Bag

Store everything in a medium-sized tote, backpack, or car organizer. Make it easy to access, even if your trunk is jammed. Update your kit every six months - check batteries, swap expired snacks, and restock anything used.

Prepared Doesn't Mean Paranoid—It Means Powerful

You may never need half of this stuff. That's the goal.

But if the day ever comes, you'll thank your past self. You'll be calm, clear-headed, and in control. And that makes all the difference.

Next Up: Final Steps on the Road to Recovery - Massage, Acupuncture, and Legal Support That Gets Results

Your journey isn't over yet. We'll guide you through the last stretch—where physical healing and legal resolution come together to bring closure, clarity, and peace.

CHAPTER 9

FINAL STEPS ON THE ROAD TO RECOVERY - MASSAGE, ACUPUNCTURE, AND LEGAL SUPPORT THAT GETS RESULTS

Healing Isn't Linear. But With the Right Tools, It's Possible.

By now, you've taken the crucial first steps—seeking care, understanding your rights, and assembling your support team. But healing after a collision isn't a one-and-done event. It's a layered process, and every layer matters.

This chapter is about rounding out your recovery: physically, emotionally, and legally. It's about going from *surviving* the crash to *fully living* again.

Let's bring it all together.

STEP 1: Don't Overlook Massage Therapy

Massage isn't just a luxury—it's a powerful healing tool. After a crash, your body holds trauma in muscles, fascia, and connective tissue. Massage helps to:

▷ Increase circulation and reduce swelling

▷ Release muscle knots and adhesions

▷ Improve range of motion

▷ Support nervous system regulation

Even one session can help your body feel safer and more mobile. A consistent schedule (1–2x per week at first) can dramatically accelerate your recovery.

STEP 2: Acupuncture for Deeper Repair

Acupuncture has been used for thousands of years—and today, modern science is catching up to its benefits.

After a collision, acupuncture can help:

▷ Calm the nervous system

▷ Decrease pain and inflammation

- ▶ Improve sleep and reduce anxiety
- ▶ Enhance your body's natural healing response

Look for a licensed acupuncturist who has experience with trauma or musculoskeletal injuries. You might be amazed how a few tiny needles can create such powerful shifts.

STEP 3: Let Your Chiropractor Coordinate Care

Think of your chiropractor as the "quarterback" of your recovery team. A good one will:

- ▶ Monitor your progress and adjust your treatment plan
- ▶ Refer you to other providers like massage therapists or acupuncturists
- ▶ Collaborate with your attorney to ensure documentation supports your legal case

You shouldn't have to navigate this alone. Let your providers talk to each other, it strengthens every part of your recovery.

STEP 4: Keep Your Legal Case Aligned with Your Healing

Your attorney should be:

- ▶ Checking in on your progress
- ▶ Keeping records of every medical visit, referral, and bill
- ▶ Advising you on when to settle—*not* pushing you to wrap up too early

You deserve full compensation—not just for your medical bills, but for your pain, your time, and your future.

This is about more than money. It's about justice. And peace of mind.

STEP 5: Stay Consistent, Even When You Feel Better

One of the biggest mistakes people make is stopping care when the pain fades.

But here's the truth: just because you feel better doesn't mean you've fully healed.

Your providers can detect subtle imbalances before they become chronic issues. Stick with your plan. Ask questions. Show up.

Healing is a marathon—not a sprint.

STEP 6: Celebrate the Wins Along the Way

Progress may be slow. Some days may feel like setbacks. But every step forward matters.

Celebrate:

- ▶ The day you sleep through the night without pain
- ▶ Your first walk without stiffness
- ▶ The moment you feel strong enough to drive again

These aren't small things. They're signs you're getting your life back.

You're Not Just Recovering—You're Reclaiming Control

We didn't write this book to impress you—we wrote it to *equip* you.

Every insight and strategy comes from decades of real-life experience—in clinics, in courtrooms, and in countless conversations with people just like you. We've helped guide hundreds through the storm. We know the path. And we know it works.

You now have tools, clarity, and confidence. And if things ever feel messy again—if the pain returns, the paperwork stacks up, or the uncertainty creeps in—flip back to any page. This isn't theory. This is your playbook.

And we're right here with you.

MOVING FORWARD WITH CONFIDENCE

Planning for the future isn't about expecting the worst. It's about giving yourself every advantage for whatever comes your way.

- ▶ **Keep Your Emergency Kit Updated**: Check contents regularly. Replace expired items, update contact info, and test batteries.
- ▶ **Stay Connected with Your Support Network**: The people who've helped you heal— your providers, attorney, family—are still part of your long-term wellness team.
- ▶ **Think Proactively**: Defensive driving courses, advanced vehicle safety features, or umbrella insurance coverage are all simple steps that can offer big protection.

Final Words

You've done more than recover, you've taken charge of your life. You're informed. Empowered. And far more prepared than most people ever will be.

And that's something to be proud of. Yours in Health and Safety,

Attorney Robert Sears & Dr. Wendy Schauer

A PERSONAL NOTE FROM ROB & WENDY

We know you didn't pick up this book for fun. You're here because something happened— maybe to you, maybe to someone you care about. You're here because life hit hard.

And we just want to say: you're not alone.

Every recommendation we've made, every section you've read - it's all rooted in real people, real recoveries, and real results. We've seen what happens when people freeze after a crash. And we've seen what's possible when they have the right information, support, and plan.

You don't have to be perfect. You just have to keep moving forward.

If you're unsure what comes next—if you want your policy reviewed, a second opinion, or someone to walk you through your options—reach out.

This book is only the beginning. Consider us your team. We're rooting for you, always.

With care,

Attorney Robert Sears & Dr. Wendy Schauer

GLOSSARY

Acupuncture: A natural healing method involving the placement of fine needles into specific points of the body to relieve pain, reduce inflammation, and support the nervous system— commonly used as part of post-collision recovery.

Adjuster (Insurance Adjuster): The person working for an insurance company who investigates your claim, assesses damage, and decides how much they're willing to pay. Not your advocate—just doing their job.

Attorney-Client Privilege: A legal protection that keeps communication between you and your attorney completely confidential.

Bodily Injury Liability (BIL): Part of your auto insurance that covers injuries you cause to someone else in a collision. It does *not* cover your own injuries.

Chiropractic Adjustment: A precise movement or thrust applied to a joint, often the spine, to restore proper alignment and improve body function. It's not cracking bones—it's restoring balance.

Chiropractic Care: A healthcare approach that focuses on restoring the body's natural alignment, function, and nervous system health—especially valuable after a crash.

Collision Coverage: Optional car insurance that pays to repair or replace your car after a crash, regardless of who was at fault.

Deductible: The amount you agree to pay out of pocket before your insurance kicks in. Higher deductibles usually mean lower premiums.

Demand Letter: A letter from your attorney to the insurance company summarizing your injuries, treatment, and requested compensation. It's the formal start of your case.

Deposition: A recorded, sworn statement you may give under oath as part of the legal process. Your attorney will be present to guide and protect you.

First Aid Kit: A simple kit with bandages, antiseptics, and medical basics. Every car should have one - especially BEFORE a crash.

Independent Medical Exam (IME): A medical exam scheduled by the insurance company— not your doctor. Often used to try to minimize your injuries or limit treatment.

Liability Coverage: Coverage that pays for damage or injuries you cause to others. It includes Bodily Injury Liability and Property Damage Liability.

Massage Therapy: Hands-on care that helps release muscle tension, improve circulation, and calm the nervous system. Often part of a smart recovery plan.

Motor Vehicle Collision: The preferred term over "accident," because it doesn't imply that the event was unavoidable or purely accidental. Words matter - especially in legal cases.

Personal Injury Protection (PIP): Insurance coverage that pays for medical expenses and lost wages regardless of fault. It's your safety net while the legal case unfolds.

Policy Limits: The maximum amount your insurance company will pay for a specific type of claim. You choose this limit when you set up your policy.

Property Damage Liability (PDL): Insurance that covers damage you cause to someone else's property (like their car or fence).

Settlement: An agreement to resolve your injury claim, usually involving a payment from the insurance company. Once accepted, your case is closed.

Soft Tissue Injury: Damage to muscles, ligaments, or tendons - not bones. Common after a crash and often underestimated by insurance companies.

Subrogation: When your own insurance company pays part of your claim, then later asks the other party's insurer to reimburse them. Sometimes they'll ask you to repay a portion from your settlement.

Treatment Gap: A period of time where you didn't receive medical care. Insurance companies love to use this to argue your injuries weren't serious.

Uninsured Motorist Coverage (UM): Protects *you* if the driver who hit you doesn't have insurance.

Underinsured Motorist Coverage (UIM): Helps when the at-fault driver's insurance isn't enough to cover your injuries.

Whiplash: A neck injury caused by a sudden, forceful back-and-forth movement. Can cause headaches, neck pain, and long-term discomfort if untreated.

INDEX

ABOUT THE AUTHORS

Attorney Robert Sears

Rob Sears is the founder and principal attorney at Sears Injury Law, PLLC, based in Puyallup, Washington. With a career dedicated to personal injury law, Rob has been advocating for the rights of injured individuals since the age of 22. His experience spans roles as a paralegal and negotiator, where he facilitated medical care and achieved significant settlements—even before earning his law degree.

As a top personal injury attorney in Washington State, Rob assists more clients each year than most of his peers. His firm recovers over $50 million annually for clients, a testament to his tenacity and deep understanding of insurance company tactics. Rob's mission is to ensure that every client not only receives justice but also the medical care and support they need to fully heal.

Rob is licensed to practice in all Washington State courts and is a sworn member of the Supreme Court of Washington. He is also an active contributor to the Washington State Association for Justice EAGLE program.

Dr. Wendy Schauer, D.C., R.K.C.

Dr. Wendy Schauer is a highly respected chiropractor with over 30 years of experience. She serves the Olympia, Washington community through her clinic, Community Chiropractic, P.S., and is the author of two acclaimed books: *The 7 Steps to Amazing Health!* and *Happy New You!: Your Roadmap to the Good Life.*

Dr. Wendy's passion is helping people reduce pain, restore function, and build stronger, healthier lives after injury. She is the recipient of the YWCA Women of Achievement Award and a finalist for the Washington State Better Business Bureau's Small Business of the Year Award. Her holistic approach to care emphasizes posture, nervous system health, and empowering patients to take control of their well-being.

She is also a Russian Kettlebell Certified (R.K.C.) instructor and holds certifications in TRX and Rocktape methods—making her uniquely skilled in both spinal health and strength restoration. Her clinic is known for its deeply personal, whole-person care model that extends beyond the adjustment table.

Together, Rob and Wendy bring decades of experience in injury law and chiropractic care to guide readers through recovery—mentally, physically, and legally—after a motor vehicle collision. Their shared mission is to remove fear, replace confusion with clarity, and give readers the tools to reclaim their health and protect their rights.

CRASH RESPONSE CHECKLIST

Tear this out or keep a printed copy in your glovebox.

🛡 In the First 30 Minutes After a Collision

☐ Stay Calm and Get to Safety
- ☐ Take a deep breath
- ☐ Check yourself and passengers for injuries
- ☐ Move vehicles off the road (if safe)
- ☐ Turn on hazard lights

☐ Call 911
- ☐ Request police AND medical/fire responders
- ☐ Stay on the line and follow dispatcher instructions

☐ Check on Others
- ☐ Check if others involved are okay
- ☐ DO NOT admit fault—only ask about injuries
- ☐ DO NOT say "I'm sorry" or discuss what happened

☐ Document the Scene
- ☐ Take photos of all vehicle damage
- ☐ Capture weather, skid marks, traffic signs/signals
- ☐ Photograph your injuries
- ☐ Use disposable camera if phone is damaged

☐ **Exchange Information**

    ☐ Other driver's name: _____

    ☐ Phone number: _____

    ☐ Address: _____

    ☐ License plate #: _____

    ☐ Insurance provider: _____

    ☐ Policy #: _____

☐ **Get Witness Info**

    ☐ Name(s): _____

    ☐ Phone(s): _____

☐ **Avoid These Mistakes**

    ☐ Don't leave the scene until cleared

    ☐ Don't post about the crash on social media

    ☐ Don't skip medical care—get checked within 24–48 hours

    ☐ Don't speak with any insurance adjuster before talking to your attorney

☐ **Call Your Chiropractor and Attorney**

    ☐ Clinic: _____Phone: _____

    ☐ Legal: _____Phone: _____